Alone in
Grief

ANRAN LIKEN

ISBN: 978-1-957956-06-0 (sc)
ISBN: 978-1-957956-07-7 (e)

Rev. date: 04/13/2022

Alone in
Grief

1

You left without an explanation why you had to go. I watched you driving away, never looking back once.

I was not sure what to do, didn't have a clue what was going on, yet you kept on driving looking round to see if the neighbours were watching—for once, no one was.

I turned going back into our home and making sure our kids were still asleep, covering them back up, thankful they didn't hear us talking, well, arguing really. I wanted to know what I had done wrong.

Life for the girls and I went on as normal—school, dancing, riding, swimming, school pantomime, etc.—but then you came back begging to come back home so we became a family again.

Life went on as usual: girls growing up, friends and boys being brought home. You were still working away, just like a normal family, or so I thought.

Then came the one: Kimberly was getting married. You weren't sure of him at first, but you grew to love him like a son; he was in the military, so we didn't get to see much of them with the moves that they made.

Then came the grandchildren. You were over the moon. Siobhan came first, then Alex. Alex was the grandson, but he became the son we couldn't have.

Victoria was still looking for Mr. Right, but she was seeing someone who may be him. She had not introduced us to him yet.

Life went on, revolving around your travels and going to see Kim, Clarkson, and the grandkids. My job was making sure that everything ran smoothly for you and our travels going to see everyone.

Then the arguments started. You didn't want to see anyone, you didn't want to go out, and then you started picking on what I was wearing, asking why I can't be more like the women you work with—makeup on, hair done, smart clothes. But I was never like that. I was always the girl-next-door type, the one who was ready to do what was needed to be done.

Your job took its toll, you needed some time off work, but they were badgering you to go back, but you got very poorly very quickly. Suddenly you were in the hospital having a test done. We were all expecting that you will need a transplant, dialysis, or both because your liver and kidneys were failing.

But no, I was called in. I took Victoria in with me. She didn't need to look after the children. We went to you in the ward; you didn't look good. We were waiting for the doctors to come. Then a nurse came to take us to a separate room. This was where we met one of the doctors treating you, Dr. Aboulous. She explained what happened and that there was nothing they can do for you, but she told us the consultant will be in to speak with us soon, as they needed something to be put in place.

Victoria went out of the room; I asked what they needed to talk to us about, and she said, "We need a DNR to be put in place."

I was shocked. It was not what we were expecting; everything started going around in my head: things that we should have done, things that were said, things that wasn't said, the memories that will be missed, seeing the grandkids grow up, seeing Vickie get married, watching other grandkids coming into the world—so many memories.

Vickie came back into the room and saw me crying and asked what had gone on.

I replied, "They want a DNR in place."

She also fell into a chair looking at me, her mouth opening and closing, not uttering any words.

Suddenly I wiped the tears from my eyes, saying, "Right, we need to call others that need to be here for this. Vickie, can you call Kim tell her she needs to get here quickly. I also need to get in touch with his sister, Aunt Samantha."

Looking at the doctor, I asked, "Can it wait till everyone is here to hear this? I know what he wanted, but I want others to agree to this too."

She replied, "Yes, we can arrange for you all to be seen this afternoon. Would that be easier?"

I nodded to reply because I can't speak, and I wasn't not sure what to think; so many thoughts were going around in my head. I took my phone out to make the calls I was really dreading having to make.

"Hi, Sam, you need to come to the Royal Hospital quickly. Jarred is not good."

Sam replied, "What do ya mean? You said he was in for tests."

"Yes, I know what I said, but things have changed very quickly. You need to get here and soon."

Looking out of the window, I wondered what life will be like without you in it. You always wanted me to stay at home, be available when you needed me to do things, pick you up from the airport or the train station, drive down to London and pick you up. I was not sure what I was going to do now.

Vickie came looking for me, making sure I was okay. "Mom, you okay? Been looking for you. Kim will be here shortly. She's getting a nan to watch the kids."

Wiping my face before I turned and not realising that I was crying, I said, "Yes, babe, I'm fine. Aunt Sam will be here soon."

We both sat in the little room not talking, just thinking about everything and nothing. Kim walked in, stopped, and looked at us both. We hugged each other and then sat down, waiting again. Kim wanted to know what was going on; we told her what we knew, which wasn't much. Time passed, but neither one of us realised until Sam came into to room with a nurse showing her in.

"Okay, so what the hell is going on? And when will this doctor be coming to see us? Let us know what is going on," she demanded.

No sooner had she finished when there was a knock at the door. In walked Dr. Aboulous and another person, whom Dr. Aboulous introduced as the consultant Mr. Tyrone. He had a sorrowful face, so we knew it was not good news that he was going to partake.

Looking around the room, he looked straight at me. "Mrs. Benedict."

I nodded my head yes because I cannot speak.

He then continued with, "We had taken your husband down on Friday to have a camera, for we needed to find where he had an internal bleeding. Now we have found this with all the blood tests that he has had done, but it is not where with the liver and kidney damage you would expect it to be. We had to resuscitate him while we were there. Now we can leave him on meds, etc., until you've decided what you want to do, but I must tell you this first: we can go in and take a further look, but that would mean him being on a ventilator and tubes coming out too. This is why we are asking for a DNR to be put in place. Do you understand all that I have said?"

We all sat in our own thoughts, the girls holding my hands. Sam was looking in disbelief at us all. I took hold of her hand, looked her in her eyes, saying, "Remember your dad, what you both went through, because your mom would not let him go."

Nodding, she remembered. Tears started to fall, for she knew what he said after their dad's death. We both turned to the consultant and instructed him to put the DNR in place; both girls, Kim and Vickie, agreed.

"Thank you, Mrs. Benedict, we will get the paperwork sorted now. We do not know how long he will live for once we stop all meds. This will depend on how strong a person is in the mind, but we will see how he does over the weekend, and if there is no change, we will stop the meds on Monday. We will now leave you so we can get Jarred moved and everything sorted." He took my hand with tears in his eyes, adding his condolences.

I thanked him with a smile, knowing that if I spoke, I would break.

2

You were moved into a side ward, a room by yourself. I was asked if I will be staying at night. My reply one word: "yes."

A cot was brought in for me. I needed to go home and get some things for my stay, not sure of what I needed. My head can't think. Vickie took over organising everything. I think she needed to be busy. I brought you in on a Thursday; by Saturday all our lives had changed forever.

Kimberly needed to get in touch with Clarkson. He was away on duty training in some desert. When his commanding officer had verified information, he was sent back home. He made it home in twenty-four hours and was dropped straight at the hospital. He cannot believe it was happening.

Welcome to the club, son. We all feel the same way, I thought.

I sat day and night watching you and cleaning your mouth, but I was not sure if I was doing it right. You get agitated by it all. Family and friends come to say their good-byes; some were heartbroken while others understood because they had been through it before.

They asked how we were feeling or me in particular, but I can't feel anything, for I was being bombarded by all the emotions at once I can't pick one particular emotion, so I just felt emptiness and numbness. I was lost and angry—everything. This was when I started to write my poetry again. It was slow at first, one or two lines. I then stopped, for it was too painful to write the feelings—everything.

We talked about anything and everything. Then it was a week later. I had a feeling it was not going to be long now, so I called Vickie and asked her to call Sam to come say her good-byes before it was too late. They all came that Saturday, a week after we agreed with the DNR.

That night I lay in the cot watching you; your breathing was getting slower and slower. I fell to sleep but not fully asleep. I was up and down most of the night, checking on you. Suddenly it was morning

On Sunday I lay on the cot watching you again, thinking I needed to get a shower before everything got busy on the ward, but something was stopping me. A voice in my head was saying, *No, wait. You need to go to him, talk to him, tell him everything is okay—that everything is all sorted.*

I also talked about your plans when you retired, and a single tear rolled down from your right eye. I wiped it away, saying it is time for you to let go. I said my own good-bye to you. As you took your last breath, I pulled the emergency cord, and everyone came running. The duty nurse checked you over, registering the time and date.

They asked if there was anyone they want to call for me, but I said no, for I had to do it myself. I need to do this one last duty. I needed to let all know that you had passed. I called the girls, then I called Sam, and lastly I called my mom and dad.

You wanted to be cremated, so we organised this. The funny thing was that your funeral was so smoothly organised. It was all the paperwork of letting your work know about your death, your pension, etc., that were taking the longest to sort.

Then I was homeless. Our landlord wanted his house back; we did have somewhere to live, but because you couldn't sign the paperwork, I lost it. With the situation I was in, I cannot get anywhere to live, so our furniture went into storage, where it stayed for seven months.

3

I moved in with Kimberly and the kids; she had an extra room. I took over the spare room, but most of our stuff was in storage, even some of my clothes, but it didn't matter, for I was losing so much weight that I had to buy new ones. But we were waiting for payments to come through. I found a little house, just big enough for me

Your money from your death in service started to come through. I gave money to the girls so they got their own places; both had gotten beautiful homes. The house I bought needed fixing up, but at least I can make it my own.

I started again with my hobbies. I opened the apps that I had closed because I didn't have time before to keep up to; this was where I met him on ViewBug. I was uploading some of my images, and an icon message popped up. "Hi, I like your images. Can we talk? I'm Ben, Benjamin Franklin. I'm a soldier in Yemen. I'm from New Jersey, America"

I was feeling lost, lonely, and, from what I had found out since your death, unloved; but I should have known by the name that it wasn't real, that it was something not right, but I wasn't getting the usual signals that something was wrong.

"Hi, thank you for liking my images. I'm Piper. How are you? It must be hard being in Yemen with all that is going on."

"Do you have a Hangouts account? I can't stay on long using this site."

"No, I don't, but I can get one. Give me a moment."

We exchanged email accounts and connected in Hangouts. He told me he was a widow, lost his wife and daughter in a car accident, that he had a son who was in military school in the UK, and that he was working with the UN.

We started to get close, and I started to have feelings for him, feelings that I thought had died with you, but I can feel them stirring. He was saying all the right things to me, what I wanted you to say to me but stopped.

Then the first request came through about money, how he wanted to get back to his son and get to know me better, so I sent money—not a lot at first.

Then he started needing larger and larger amounts. When I checked, I have lost £50,000. Then he was talking about diamonds that he was smuggling out of Yemen. I was thinking what the hell was going on. How did it get to wanting to meet up to this.

Then he was in prison because he had been caught with the diamonds. Then the demands were getting even bigger, and I suddenly realised that I was being scammed. I had tried everything to stop talking to him. I blocked him on everything, but forgot about my email. He had it so he could get to me through my emails.

Always begging and pleading, saying he was going to die in this place that he was in, I reminded him of what he had done to get where he was but at the same time not really believing that he was in such a place, believing that he was in a house nice and cosy, while talking to me about being in a prison in Dubai, then it's Turkey—all the time asking for money. I don't even think that the image he sent me was really him.

I needed to get away from everything. It was all crowding in on me. I can't breathe anymore. I panicked. Kim took me to the doctors, and I was given medication to help with everything

I booked a ticket to go away for a week, taking my camera with me. I went to Scotland. Driving was doing me some good. I was feeling calmer by each mile that I was taking away from it all.

I arrived at my hotel, and there it was again: a message from him asking what he can do to prove that he was who he said he was. I ignored it for a few days, but still he was messaging me more and more about proving who he was. so I told him I wanted a video call, FaceTime, or Skype call—a face-to-face thing—to prove it is him in the image he sent, not really believing that he will do this.

Moments later, I got a missed call. He then messaged me asking why I didn't answer. I was telling him I didn't know he was going to call, so he called back, and there he was, the man in the image. And I thinking, *What the hell, what do I believe, or not believe anymore. Why is this happening? Why?* I was so confused, wanting to believe but not wanting to believe.

He was still asking for more money, now begging, pleading for more and more. Then he asked me to buy a diamond certificate from Kimberley Clark for these are the people who will give you certificates to sell precious metals and gems. It cost more than £200,000.

I was shocked. I cannot believe I was being asked, but then I thought, *Yes, you can. This is getting really stupid now.*

I messaged him back telling him to go away and to leave me alone. I wanted nothing to do with what he had done, nothing to do with the stones, nothing. I asked him to just go and leave me alone. I blocked him.

While all this was going on, I was talking with Flynn, who was so different to the man in his movies, and I was thinking, *How can he and the other guy I was talking to be so different? How did I get here? How can I stop talking, but I'm so lonely.*

4

Then it was your birthday, and I saw one of my favourite actors' image on Facebook. I put a comment on it. I think it was an image where he was looking lost, and I commented, "Lost soul."

Then he messaged me, "Hi, Piper, this is Flynn Masters. Why do you say 'lost soul' on my image?"

I had to read this a few times to understand what was going on, but then I thought, *What the hell—is it or isn't.*

So I answered, "Hi, Flynn, nice to hear from you. My comment was because you do look like a lost soul in that image. I've also noticed that your smile does not reach your eyes anymore."

Then nothing came back, so I didn't think anything of it from then on. Then a few days after your birthday, I woke up to a few messages from Flynn asking different things. I answered his questions. He also answered mine.

"Are you married?"

"I like this image of you."

"You are beautiful."

"Do you have kids?"

"What do you think of my movies?"

"Tell me, which one is your favourite?"

"Which one did you last watch?"

I knew he was from Australia, but I didn't know if he lived there or if he was living in America, where the movies seem to be made nowadays. I tried to answer his questions.

"I'm a widow, just lost my husband."

"Thank you for liking my image. This was taken at a friend's wedding."

"As to me being beautiful, well, I just think I am ordinary, nothing special."

"Yes, I have two daughters."

"I like all your movies."

"No, I couldn't pick a favourite."

"Your last one, the rom-com *She Blow Me Away*. I thought this was really funny, and it suited my mood at the time. It made me cry with laughter. This was just before I lost my husband."

"What about you, do you have any movies in the mix? You seem to bring out two to three movies straight after each other."

But at the same time I was aware of his privacy, not wanting to step on his toes by asking too many personal questions.

I sat in the bedroom at Kim's, and I was thinking, *Why would someone like him contact me, calling me all the names under the sun, for believing that anything so fantastic could or would happen to the likes of me? Get your head out of the clouds, girl.*

My life was in turmoil with all that was going; the messages were still coming thick and thin, no matter how many times I blocked them. Ben was becoming annoying with his constant begging, pleading, "I'm crying here on bended knees, God made you an angel."

And yet Flynn was nothing how I would expect a movie star to be; he was so down to earth, but that could also be how a great of an actor he was though.

He asked if I had ever been to Australia, and I told him no, for if I did go to Australia, I would not want to come back to the UK. He laughed at this while asking if I would like to go out and visit. I said yes, I would but not sure if I should.

He then asked if I'd been to America. I told him yes, but for a short visit.

We went that time when you were working, and I asked if I could come with you. I spent my time alone taking my images.

I told him I was planning on a tour that would take in a few countries around the world, for I thought I needed to do this to get myself sorted properly to get over losing you. All I had ever known was looking after the girls and you, being there for you all or trying to be there.

It has now been a few months since you went, and things seem to be getting a bit heavy with Flynn. I just don't know what to believe anymore. All that we knew when growing up as kids had all changed. It is all done with media, on apps. No one calls each other anymore. It is all so confusing. I found myself crying because it all built up the pressure of having to go through all the memories. I kept feeling guilty that I was betraying you, but then others told me you were the one that passed, not me. I was still a youngish woman who can find love again, but I don't know.

It all came crashing in sometimes, just wanting to curl up and have a good cry. The messaging was getting out of hand now with more and more wanting to join, but they were all saying they are "Flynn Masters."

I talked to Flynn himself, and he kept telling me to block them, but they still kept finding my email. I think I have had about fifteen trying to connect, all wanting the same thing—money. I often wondered if my media pages had a light bulb blinking on it somewhere saying "money," so I closed them all down, stopped using them, but I used this for my craftwork to sell, so I had to open them up again. But I made it so no one can get my email unless they go and look further on my pages.

5

The house was coming along, just waiting for planning on the extension to the kitchen. Fires were finally in; hopefully I can get someone in to do plastering for me. That is one job I do not fancy doing myself. I need it doing right, just needed to make it a home and not constantly living in a building site, had someone come around, but I was still waiting on quotes.

I was getting that pressure feeling in my chest again. I know what it meant though. I just needed to get out go for a walk or drive somewhere to walk. Sometimes this helped; sometimes it didn't.

Flynn was asking me to visit him in America, but I was not sure, but something kept telling me I had to go. It was like a little gremlin was in my brain telling to go, so I booked a flight to America.

I didn't tell anyone yet, for I didn't want them to try and talk me out of going. For the more it gets closer to me travelling, I am feeling more and more calm, not as panicky, but the girls didn't seem to like that I was getting on with my life. Over the last few weeks all they wanted to do was argue over whether I should or should not, but they had to realise that my life was finally starting. I didn't have to stay at home waiting for your calls to come and collect you anymore.

It was getting more tense with Kim and Victoria. I was feeling more and more stifled by them wanting me to not carry on with my life. I'd asked numerous times for help with doing things in my home, so my sister was coming over to help between her my mom and dad.

We had done so much in five weeks: three bedrooms, landing, hallway, stairs, and lounge all decorated—even built a dressing room in my bedroom.

During the first week of decorating, there was a massive argument with the girls over what I still don't know or even understand. They came around to my house screaming and shouting like banshees refusing to come in of off the street. I grabbed them both by the arms shoving them out of my home, telling each of them to get out of my house.

Kim grabbed for my hair, but my police training took over, so I got her hair, turning it so she was shoved out of my home. I managed to get them out of the house, locking the door behind them. I broke down, saying, "I'm not going through being controlled again, not by my daughters. I've had enough."

I talked to one of my counsellors about what happened, and I was advised of going away for a month, telling me I needed a complete break from everything, but I cannot afford a month away.

Finally, the week before I flew out to America, my little house was coming together. All I had to do was work on the dining room and kitchen, but I was not sure if I was going ahead with the extension. We will have to wait and see.

Life is funny at times, for you were telling people that all our problems were because of me, but now everyone was seeing that it was you making things up to make me look bad. I never cheated or looked at another man while we were together, and when I started talking to other men when you passed, all hell was breaking loose.

I shouldn't be doing this. I shouldn't want to be with another man. I shouldn't even be thinking this way, but where was all this when you were skirting around on me? Where was all this anger? There was none of it, because you were telling people that it was in my head. Whenever we were in company, you were all over me, but what they didn't realise was that when they left, you never even came anywhere near me.

The messages were still coming through all from different people; some were scammers wanting money. I was starting to see these by now but not before I lost a lot of money.

I was talking to a lot of different people, yes. A lot were men looking for women—some for a serious relationship, others for extramarital cheating on spouses. But I didn't do this. I never have, and I never will. I'm not built this way.

I looked at the money, and I realised I've lost it all. I've just got enough for my trip. I always did say I never wanted money. I just wanted your time, but I guess that never sunk into your brain.

Well, Flynn was getting really excited about me going over to see him. He told me there are a lot of places he wanted to take me. I was booked into a hotel for two weeks, but for my own safety more than anything, for I really don't know if he was for real or just someone looking for a quick buck, but whichever it is, I was going to enjoy myself, for I have never done anything like this in my life. I kept telling myself it was a new adventure, a new life, a new chapter, a new book to write.

Things were not what they always seem to be at first. It felt as though he didn't remember talking or messaging with me, but with more talking, we found that we have a lot in common, the very same with our conversations from our messages. We were sitting in one of the many lounge areas at my hotel. I can hear cameras clicking, people whispering, some quiet, some not so quiet.

"Oh, who is that?"

Someone answered, "Flynn Masters."

"Oh, who is he with? Does anyone know her name?"

I asked him if this was annoying him because he was looking angry. He looked at the concierge, who came over. Next, he looked at the people with cameras, and others stopping to look at us were moved on. He took my hand, and we moved to go through a door that was being held open for him.

It led into a car park area, but there was only one car parked. We seemed to be walking towards it, but I hesitated for a moment, which made Flynn turn, saying, "We are not going anywhere. It is so we can talk more privately."

I nodded my head because I cannot speak. I kept thinking, *I'm with Flynn Masters. He is holding my hand, and it feels so right.*

We got into his car. The windows were tinted black so no one can really see inside, not with it in the dark parking area

"Now this is better. We can talk without people overhearing what we are talking about. Now my apologies for being distant. Yes, I remember our messages. I just didn't want the media knowing how long we had been conversing. Can I just say this? I have been dying to say this since I walked through and saw you waiting for me. You are so much more beautiful in person. There is a glow about you as people are watching you, and you don't ever realise this."

I sat looking into his eyes, listening to his voice. It was even more sexy in person. All I wanted to do was kiss him, but I stopped reaching for him.

"So, you do remember our conversations then? You just didn't want the people around to know about this, why? Are you ashamed of talking with me?"

A look of anger came into his eyes. He turned away. I went to get out of the car, but Flynn took hold of my hand tighter. He looked at my hand, which looked so tiny against his.

"I want you, to be with you more than you know. I am trying very hard not to take you at this very moment. I want to make you mine. I told you in my messages how I felt about you, my feelings have not changed, you see what we celebrities have to go through. Would you mind if you move into my home while you are here? You can still keep your hotel if this will make you feel safe somewhere for you to come back to if you need time."

"Okay, I will pack a small case for a few days at least. Then if it doesn't work out, I can return, yes."

He looked at me not sure what to say, but then he nodded his head. "Yes, if you want to return."

We got out of his car, but this time there was an escort to my room. I packed my small case with clothes I can use for a few days, looking around wondering if I had forgotten something when Flynn asked, "You got a bathing suit?"

I replied, "Yes, I have a few."

"Bring them all."

Closing my case, I went to retrieve my bag with my wash things and basic makeup.

"Add this to go." Flynn took my bags.

We moved out of my room, walking down the corridor. A few people were coming and going from their rooms, but Flynn never saw them looking at him. I understood more about what he was saying when he kept asking if I could tolerate how people stare at me, but with the escort, we moved to his car quickly.

On the journey to his home, we didn't talk, but I thought this was because of the people in the car who seemed to be doing all the talking, mostly about the projects that they had going on.

Flynn took my hand. I turned looking at my hand in his. Then looking at him, he smiled. I squeezed his hand letting, him know I was okay. He then turned to involve me in the conversation.

I must admit I didn't pay too much attention to where we were travelling. I'd been to America before and was amazed by the buildings, but LA is so much different, but again I never took anything in of the buildings we travelled past. I finally looked out of the window, and the photographer in me was awestruck by the beauty—the sea, the hills, the woodlands.

We were travelling round winding roads. I soon got disorientated. Then we were pulling into a drive, then garage. The others in the car left, going in different ways before the garage doors closed. We didn't get out of the car straight away. I was about to ask that if he was not sure about it, then I can always go back to the hotel.

He turned and took my hand again, saying, "I understand that this is not normal for you, and I will understand if you want me to take you back to your hotel, but please, just give us—you and I—a chance."

I replied, "Yes, I am nervous about all of this, but if I were not sure about us, I would not have gotten into your car. I'm not a little girl. I'm grown woman. Yes, it has been awhile since I was with a man, the way we may get together, but I am going through this door that has opened up for me."

He got out of the car, and before I can get out from my side the door, it was opened. I was still in my seat. He took me so gently, taking hold of my face, saying, "I've been wanting to do this since I saw you sitting waiting so patiently."

Then he kissed me softly at first but made it deeper. I moved closer, feeling him between my legs. Pulling away, we were both breathing heavily. I slid out of the car while Flynn got my bags out of the boot.

I was thinking there was no way I would be going back to my hotel. My legs were like jelly, but I managed to stand and walk into his home.

7

I wasn't sure what to expect of his home, but it was nice for a man smiling to myself. There were wide open spaces into the lounge area that opened onto a terrace. There were grasses down to the edge of a cliff with a view of the sea, amazing view of the sea really.

"Come this way. I will show you the bedrooms. You can choose which one you would like. Then I will show you the rest."

There are four bedrooms, all with their own bathrooms; each one was big enough to fit my lounge, kitchen, and office in. I noticed that he was no longer carrying my bags. I never noticed when or where he had put them, so I said, "Wherever you have laid my bags down, I guess that is where I'll be staying."

I saw the little sheepish smile come onto his face but noticed him removing it when he realised I was watching, so I laughed, saying, "If you wanted me to stay with you in your room, you should have just said. We Yorkshire lasses love plain talking."

He laughed one of those laughs that come from the stomach, saying, "You are like a breath of fresh air."

"Well, you must have been in some smelly places if I'm a breath of fresh air."

"Come, get changed. We are going into the pool."

"You've got a pool?"

"Babe, this is California. Almost everyone has a pool."

I went back to his bedroom, which was my favourite room among the others. The colours were exactly what I would have chosen. The texture, feel of the room were so welcoming that I wouldn't want to leave it.

The pool was a good size, not too small and not too big, exactly right for play and serious swimming.

He handed me a robe, wrapping it around me. We went to the pool area. It felt like a tropical spa with the pool, steam room, sauna, plants. I cannot name some palm trees, potted plants—all with beautiful colours.

I can hear water trickling. Turning around, Flynn was under a waterfall that was an outside shower. Okay so when in Rome, do what Romans do; so I got under the water, which was warm. Afterwards, I dove into the water of the pool, it felt really good to be back swimming, not realising that Flynn was standing and watching as I swam up and down his pool. I stopped out of breath, panting. I looked into his green eyes while he was smiling at me.

"What?" I asked.

He just smiled, getting in beside me. "You were telling the truth that you could swim."

I laughed because I knew he didn't believe me. "Do the women you've been involved with before do not swim?"

"Ha-ha, not the way you've just done, no, they don't. It is mainly getting wet, then sunning on a lounger," he replied.

"Oh, I can do this also, but I like to read a book too, but I've never been anywhere like this though."

We talked more, swam even more, before I said, "I've had enough. I'm looking like prune."

We both got out, drying. And he asked if I would like a drink: alcohol, fruit juice, coffee, tea, or water.

"Can I have fruit juice? But I can get it if you tell me where everything is. You don't have get it for me," I said, not realising he was making it fresh.

He brought out of a fridge that I didn't realise was there. I never noticed the bar area just off to the right of the pool; the fruit that was on the countertop looked gorgeous, some I know while others not so much: pineapples, pawpaw, guava, strawberries, cherries, and many others.

"Please don't put strawberries in mine or alcohol, for I'm allergic to both."

"Yes, I remember this from our messages."

I was watching him how quickly he cut the fruit up to go into the machine at the counter. He put a few other ingredients into my drink, pouring it over with crushed ice, handing it to me. It tasted amazing. I felt so energised.

Smiling at me, he said, "It is good, yes?"

I just nodded my head, taking a bigger drink, not realising that some of the juice had trickled out of my glass and trailed down my chin round onto my neck. He was watching this, but I was not paying attention. When I realised that it had trickled, I put my glass down, and I reached for some tissue, but Flynn grabbed my hand before I could reach it. Looking into my eyes, he moved to lick where the trail of juice had just taken.

Holding on to his arms, my hands fell to his waist. I pulled him closer but then stopped. He took my lips, moving closer, but we heard voices. I pulled away, but he held me even closer.

In walked his ex-girlfriend, talking as though they were still together, but I knew this to be not true. She stopped talking and walking at the same time.

"Who the hell is this?" she demanded. She demanded to know what was going on while walking around to where we both were. I was sitting. Flynn was standing in front of me, not saying a word and just letting her rant.

"What the hell is going on? I'm going to rip your hair out, bitch. How dare you try coming between my husband and me."

I tried to move from the stool I had sat down on, but Flynn put his hand on my arm, saying, "Please stay. Don't go."

I can only nod my head, for I was angry, but he saw this and kissed me full in front of this manic woman, whom I knew was no longer his girlfriend. Flynn and Olivia were never married even after the years they were together. They never came close to getting married. I now understand why. I was shaking with what she was saying about Flynn and me.

He then turned to me. "Don't, babe, this is what she's wanting, but please allow me."

Turning around, he looked at Olivia not moving away from me, but unbeknown to me, he had pressed a button, and two security people came walking out to the pool area.

He asked, "Why was she allowed into my house? I gave direct instruction that she was never allowed in this house. Now she wants to insult my guest."

Looking towards Olivia, he said, "You, you listen to me. You left me, you aborted our child, you made that choice without even telling me. I then find out that you cheated on me and said baby was not even mine. You made these choices. You, you wanted the break. You wanted to separate. I gave you what you wanted. Now leave me alone.

I have moved on and this woman here"—pointing at me, turning to kiss me also—"she has shown me more about what it is to be in love, what it is to have someone love you without conditions. Now leave this house, or I will call the police to have you removed." He nodded to the security people.

They moved to lead Olivia out of the house, still ranting and screaming that she will go to every tabloid to tell her story and sell it to whoever will listen, she said as for showing me around the rest of his home it is forgotten.

8

"Oh my goodness, that was Olivia DeMarco, your girlfriend of what, nine to ten years, but I always wondered why you guys never married. Well, now I know why. Was all this just recent, the cheating and the baby?"

I saw the sadness in his eyes. They tear up. I took hold of his hand, squeezing it to show that I understood. I was sure he didn't want to talk about it, but then he started to talk with a catch in his voice.

"Yes, the latter you spoke of about, the baby, yes, but the cheating has or had been going on for a number of years. I think that is why I never asked her to marry me. Oh, don't get me wrong, when we first got together, I wanted nothing more than to marry her, but whenever I went to buy a ring, something always stopped from me getting that ring."

He stopped talking. I can see he was struggling with what he had just told me.

"Flynn, we cannot change what happened in both of our pasts, but we can move forward, walking through our fear of thinking this might happen again, but not everyone is built to cheat. I know I'm not, but I understand if you want to take me back to my hotel."

Taking a step back, he turned to me and said, "Are you mad, woman? You have kept me sane these last few months. I never thought I would find a woman who has a pure heart like yours. Olivia and I have been separated for eighteen months now, and I have never looked at another woman, but your comment made me . . . made me stop. I had to talk to you. It was as though someone or something was telling me to talk with you. Hence, where we are today. Please don't let her take you away from me also."

I got off the stool, reaching for his hands. I took hold of him, asking him to look at me. He hesitated at first but turned looking me full in the face. I saw his pain, his fear in those eyes, his beautiful green blue-grey eyes. "No one can take me away from you but you. Only you can make me leave."

Taking my face between his hands and pulling me closer, he kissed my forehead, saying,

"How did I find an angel like you? You make me feel like there is nothing I cannot do when I'm with you." Taking hold of me properly, I put my arms around him, thinking it was so amazing, my head resting up on his chest, listening to his heart beating.

After Olivia was escorted away from his home, it changed that day; the afternoon was very subdued. Flynn seemed to be thinking about and apologising for the intrusion of Olivia.

Looking at him, I asked, "Why? Why are you apologising. Do you still want her? For most of this afternoon, you've not said much. You have been very quiet. Look, I think it is best if I go back to my hotel. It seems you have a lot to sort out about your feelings for Olivia."

Walking away, I turned. "You need to be alone to maybe download and process all that went on this morning. After that, we can go to my hotel and collect the rest of my clothes. I can pay my bill also. I'll try to get an early flight back home."

I never made it to the door of his house. Flynn grabbed me by my waist, picking me up. He carried on to his bedroom; we ended up lying on his bed, kissing each other all the way through while he was walking to his room. This continued. We don't have much clothing to take off, for we were still in our swimwear.

He stopped, hesitated in what he was doing; laying his head on my breasts, I moved my hands to his hair, the soft texture of this silky strands. I ran my fingers through it, caressing his scalp, looking up from where he lay.

"I'm sorry, I just want you so much, and with what you said, this made me so angry, but I don't want our first time together to be in anger."

Laughing nervously, I replied, "Oh, so you think I'm easy?" But I took hold of his face, for I see the pain almost coming into his eyes and started kissing him, hoping he will understand that I was feeling the same way about him.

Things got a bit heated, but we never went very far. Flynn stopped. "No, not yet, I want you, yes, but not yet."

We showered tougher, which in itself was just as much if not quite making love. Watching him dress was just as much as a turn-on as watching him undress, thinking to myself, *Down, girl, put those thoughts away for later.*

I got dressed, putting shorts and a T-shirt on with an over shirt over the top, and I slipped on a pair of flip-flops. I walked out of the room, for watching Flynn was giving me some rather dirty thoughts, and if I didn't get away for five minutes, I would be jumping them bones.

We returned to my hotel to gather the rest of my things.

9

I cannot believe that I had been here a week. I was dreading getting my flight back home. I had not checked any of my phones, but I really should if only to find out about home.

Finding my phones, there were a few messages from home asking if all was going okay and why haven't I messaged back, etc. I dealt with these first. Then I checked on my emails, which were dealt with yet again quickly. My other phone was a different matter. I thought about changing my number, for every time I was blocking Benjamin, he was just getting another number and making contact to my email address for this phone that I closed down months back.

I thought, *I will have to sort this when I get back home.* I still can't believe I gave so much money to help him, to get him free of what I believed to be true, but I was not in a very good place. Maybe I will have to take this further.

Flynn came walking into the room. Well, no, let's say he came crashing into the room, raging into his phone. He noticed that I was in the room, but I made a move to leave so he can have some privacy. He took hold of my hand before I could leave, shaking his head no; wanting that I stay, he finished his call quickly.

"You will not believe what I have just had to deal with. Olivia is trying to take me to court, citing that you were the course of our breakup."

Looking at him in disbelief, I replied, "But I have proof with our messages that we never knew each other during your time with her.

Also, we only connected a few months back, well, six months if you want specifics. Well, let her, I have nothing to hide."

Huffing out a deep breath, he looked at me, pulling me towards him, holding in his arms resting his head on top of mine. "Where did you come from, that fierce look in your eyes wanting to take on whatever she throws at us?"

Saying into his chest, I replied, "I am just me."

Moving slightly apart and looking into each other, searching and finding, he kissed me gently at first. Then I pushed harder, wanting more than just kisses. He then pulled away, wagging his finger saying no, I smiled, knowing it was just as hard for him also.

Moving to sit down again, he asked, "Do you still want to go out for something to eat with what Olivia has threatened?"

I replied with, "Why wouldn't we go out? Why do we have to let her spoil our evening?"

Then realisation hit me. "Oh, you mean that she's gone public with all this? Okay, yes, why not? Then you can see how I behave in public, and you can get a feel whether I will be okay with it all."

Reaching over, he took my hand, kissed my fingers, smiling. We made a move to go out. We went to his garage, and we climbed into one of his vehicles. Pressing a gadget, the doors rolled open. There were flashes of light. Flynn cursed, realising that we were in the midst of a frenzy.

He was angry. I can feel it growing in him. He went to get out of the car, but I stopped him, taking hold of his hand

"Kiss me like I'm your last breathe." He looked confused at first.

Then it hit him. "You do know that by doing this, you will have them following you everywhere."

I nodded at him, and he shook his head. Then his hand brushed through my hair. His other hand was taking hold of my face. Reaching over the gear lever, we kissed, and with my closed eyes, I can see the flash as the images were taken.

"Thank you." We both said to each other without neither of us realising how tense we were feeling until that kiss. We were driving away because we had just given them the story. Now the fight was on to see who could get it published first.

10

That second week was so surreal. We were followed everywhere by people with cameras, phones with cameras—all taking pictures, videos, etc. Flynn got angry at times, but he never understood why I just ignored it all and just enjoyed all that we were doing: the sanctuary for horses and donkeys, the walks and bike rides in the hills—so many that I can't remember but the memories will last me a life time.

We returned from one of our rides. It was a few days after the kiss. People were waiting in Flynn's office; they didn't look very friendly. I learned that they were his management team.

Holding my hand, he pulled me into the office saying hello to everyone in the room. "Can I introduce Piper, Piper Benedict."

A rather looking stoutly gentleman replied very strongly with an angry voice and a smirk on his face, "Yes, we know it is in all the tabloids. What is the meaning of this? You said she was just a thing you had to work through, an itch to scratch."

Flynn was watching me, not really looking at the group. He knew that the words spoken hurt me, but I hid the pain from the group, turning at the last word spoken with anger on his face.

"Roger, please be very careful what you say. You are in my home, and I will not have anyone insulted here. Do we understand that? Piper, please let me apologise for what you have just heard. It was uncalled for and not necessary, but first, before you all start in on what has transpired, I want a legal proceeding to start against Olivia. This clown of a show with the media is her doing, but if it was not for this woman here, I would have hit a few people."

I can feel everyone looking at me, wondering, *Why is she still in the room?*

Why has he not told me to go? I was wondering the same thing.

"Mr. Masters, before we start, may I ask if Ms. Piper goes from the room while we discuss this situation?"

"Milea, no, I'm sorry. Piper is not leaving this room while we discuss her also. She does have a right to know what will happen with this situation as you so delicately put it. I will say this much about this woman that you all seem to be pointing daggers at of how to cope with the media, and you know there is quite a few out there who could learn from her. But from what you see in the images, I'm sure soon the media will soon realise it as well."

Looking at Flynn who was still holding my hand, I squeezed it. He turned. I said, "Can I say something, please."

He nodded.

"Mr. Roger, Ms. Milea, everyone—I understand how you are feeling. I get it. You think what the hell does she know about all of this, what does she know about dealing with the media, etc. You're right, I don't know anything about the media in the sense that you have too, but I am a human being, and so are they, but they also have a job to do. Yes, they can be bullies about what or how they go about getting some of their images, but I have always treated people the way I want to be treated. I can only be me around people. I cannot be pretentious, just myself."

During my little speech, there were a few who looked down, not looking me in the eye because I had just said what they—if not all—were thinking. But this broke the tension in the room.

Flynn then said, "Look, guys, let's take this in to the kitchen. I need a drink of coffee anyway, and since this lady came into my life,

I need food. She works me to death." He was laughing going out of the room as everyone followed.

A press release appeared the next day stating that I was not the course of Flynn's and Olivia's breakup. There were two pictures with the release: one of Flynn and Olivia with a tear down the middle, the other of Flynn and I. But it was one that I had not seen before, both of us looking into each other's eyes. It looked like it was a side shoot, but it captured the love we both have for each other.

Looking at this image made me realise that, yes, I do love this man, for he is funny, loving, kind, honest, truthful, caring. I now know why I never saw him for the celebrity that he was. I had always loved him.

All too soon, I have to pack my bags to get my flight home. I realised that I had not checked my phones since last week. There were a million messages, mostly from family wanting to know what was going on due to the media and the press release. I let everyone know that I was okay and will tell them all when I get back home.

Flynn walked into our bedroom and saw that I'd been crying. He just took me into his arms and held me, saying, "I don't want to let you go, but I know you have to, but I will come find you soon. There are things we need to discuss, but I want to see where you live, see you in your environment. Do you understand me."

I can't speak; my throat choked with wanting to cry, but I nodded my understanding on what he meant.

11

Our drive to the airport was quiet, both immersed on our different thoughts. I was thinking if I will ever meet with him again and hoping that I would. I was not sure about Flynn's, but I was hoping just maybe he was thinking the same.

He drove to a valet parking area that I had not seen when I first landed. We walked towards the airport. My cases were taken inside to check in. We were walking into the airport, and—*wham*—there were flashes of lights, and questions were being shouted. Flynn had warned me about this and that we may have to answer some questions, some were about Olivia, but Flynn closed them down quickly, which turned the questions to what we had been doing.

But one asked a question that I was not expecting. "When is the wedding, Flynn?"

We both turned to each other. I was laughing with a twinkle in my eyes. Flynn was doing the same, but he had a serious look in his eyes, almost as though he was thinking of something completely different.

Turning to the media, he said, "You will have to watch this space."

We walked away, with him almost dragging me. "Flynn, please slow down. I've only got short legs."

He stopped dead, and I almost crashed into him, but he steadied me before I hit into him. He had a serious look in his eyes, as if he was trying to figure something out but not sure what it was.

We made our way to the check-in desk. My passport and tickets were dealt with quickly. The girl was not taking her eyes of off Flynn. I

had a little smile on my face because I knew what she was thinking—
what a hunk, or possibly something more. But Flynn did not even
notice her. He was playing with my hair; he never left my hair alone.

"Come, we can go to one of the lounges, get a bit of peace, plus I
don't want to let you go yet."

He took me to an area I did not see when we walked into the
airport. It was a lounge, almost like the one farther into the airport
but a bit more posh. He showed a card. We were passed through into
the lounge.

We talked constantly. There were people in the lounge who knew
Flynn; they came to talk, looking at me wanting to know who I am,
but Flynn never told them.

Then my flight was called. I was taken to a different room, this
time to get my flight. We said our good-byes. I was trying not to cry,
but it was very hard. Flynn gave me one last kiss on my forehead,

Not realising that I was in the VIP lounge for celebrities, I was
the last to board the plane. I was also moved into first class without
me knowing.

I showed my ticket to the air hostess. "Ah, Ms. Benedict, come this
way. There is also a package attached to this seat, ma'am."

Following her down to my seat, I saw what she meant. There was
the biggest flower arrangement with a card. I started laughing, taking
the card, and turning, I asked, "Where can these be put for safely?"

"We can leave them in the next seat, ma'am. This is not taken."
She moved them so I can sit down. I was offered champagne, which
I refused. I asked if there was any fruit juice. I was given choices. I
chose a tropical juice.

The captain announced that we were getting ready to take off. The seat belt sign went on. I fastened my belt, waiting for the lift. Then we were airborne. I read the card once we had levelled out.

"Piper, you are an amazing woman. You taught me so much, of how to be just human and not to take things too seriously. I love you always. We will meet again soon, my love. Always, Flynn."

12

Landing back in the UK were just the same people rushing to collect their bags. I was walking along not really paying attention to the others around me. Then bright light flashed on my face.

I was blinded for a moment. Someone has taken a photo with their phone. Blinking so I can see again, suddenly there were people around me while I was trying to get to passport control.

They were all asking the same questions.

"Were you the woman with Flynn Masters?"

During all this, the flowers were getting heavy in my arms. Someone must have said something to Security, for the next thing I knew, I was being escorted to passport control, which was good.

I didn't have to wait very long to get through. In my head, I was thinking and laughing to myself, *What the hell.*

Collecting my cases, I made my way out to my car. Walking through to the car park, the airport was busy with people coming and going on holidays and business trips. Making my way around them to the exit, I realised I was being followed.

It was a little girl. I stopped and asked if she was okay. She nodded her head, and then she asked, "Can I have your autograph?"

I ask her why, and she replied, "You are the lady that Flynn Masters is going to marry."

Looking at her sincere face, I took the pen and paper she was still holding out and signed it. She looked at it, saying, "Thank you, Piper." She then ran back to where she came from.

Walking on to my car, I was thinking. *Marry, marry—since when?*

I found my car and loaded my cases, and his flowers took the front seat. Pushing the trolley to the trolley park, I was still thinking, *Marry, marry.*

My drive home was uneventful, thank goodness, but I was thinking that I needed to sort the situation out with my money. I needed to get in touch with the police to try and stop others losing their money too. If I had been in a better place, I don't think they would have gotten any money from me, but that cannot be changed now. It was gone. I just have to get them stopped.

I was pulling into the driveway of my little cottage. It was good to be home, but it felt even more empty now that I know you're not waiting for me to return. I didn't get out of my car. I sat with my head on the steering wheel, crying at it all out that I was never going to see you again, but I have the memories.

Taking a deep breath, I got out of my car, taking everything into the house. Mail was piled up at back of the door. After gathering the mail off the floor, I started turning the lights on, moving through the house just to make it more lighter, for it had turned dark outside with clouds, threatening to rain, which suited my mood.

Mail was in my home office, and I was thinking to myself, *I'll deal with this later.*

But one caught my eye. It had my bank emblem on it, so I opened it, falling down into my chair. It was telling me that my funds were gone. I was wondering how.

Then reading further, they were telling me to get in touch with them and also the police. I was put in touch with Action Fraud or something. I was a bit flummoxed, can't believe I'd been so stupid, but with all that had been going on, yes, I can believe it.

Grief is a strange situation to go through, especially when it is either your husband or wife who passed away. What was your life is gone. It is turned upside down. Everything blends into one, and you feel as though you are in a tunnel with no ending.

Well, all details were given to the police. Now just have to wait till they run their investigation. Hopefully what they find might and could help others, but there is more that I can do also. Surely, there are more out there that are possibly in the same situation that I found myself in but are too embarrassed to come forward, afraid of being called stupid or with more hurtful words.

Grief is a funny thing. It is an emotion we avoid talking about, but we all go through it at some point in our life, all in our own different way.